RITUALS

— FOR —

EVERY DAY

Simple Tips and Calming Quotes
to Refresh Your Mind, Body and Spirit

RITUALS FOR EVERY DAY

Text by Miranda Moore

An Hachette UK Company
www.hachette.co.uk

Vie Books, an imprint of Summersdale Publishers Ltd
Part of Octopus Publishing Group Limited
Carmelite House
50 Victoria Embankment
LONDON
EC4Y 0DZ
UK

www.summersdale.com

Printed and bound in China

ISBN: 978-1-80007-675-4

Substantial discounts on bulk quantities of Summersdale books are available to corporations, professional associations and other organizations. For details contact general enquiries: telephone: +44 (0) 1243 771107 or email: enquiries@summersdale.com.

INTRODUCTION

A ritual is a series of actions performed with reverence and awareness. With practice, these actions could enrich your life and give your days clarity and purpose. Through repetition, your mind and body learn to recognize a sequence of simple actions, preparing you mentally and physically for whatever you wish to achieve. This book introduces a range of nurturing rituals and explores the significant benefits they afford the mind, body and spirit. Inspiring, mindful quotes sprinkled throughout this book set the tone for you to make the very most of your practice.

RITUALS ARE THE
FORMULAS BY WHICH
HARMONY IS RESTORED.

Terry Tempest Williams

WHERE THERE'S PEACE, ALLOW IT TO REIGN.

Chidera Eggerue

WHAT ARE
RITUALS?

A ritual is an act of self-care carried out mindfully and with reverence. Rituals are generally sequences of actions performed in a set pattern, at a particular time or for a particular purpose, with an attitude of respect and dignity. With repetition, they often take on a meditative or even sacred quality. Rituals also have a clear purpose or intention behind them, and mostly take just a few minutes to perform. Choosing rituals that suit your lifestyle and mindset – or perhaps help you to overcome some specific obstacles – will help you to live each day with calmness and purpose.

Rituals can be tailored to your unique circumstances and needs. There are rituals for particular times of day; rituals for processing emotions or creating mental space; some for boosting energy or morale, embracing new challenges or promoting a particular outcome; others for reaching acceptance or finding closure; and rituals for acknowledging special events or milestones.

Often, top sportspeople, actors and presenters perform idiosyncratic rituals before they begin playing, performing or speaking. These familiar sequences help to calm their nerves and prepare them for whatever they are about to face.

EVEN THE MOST
ENORMOUS THINGS
CAN BE CUT UP
INTO TINY PARTS.

Laura Imai Messina

MEDITATION SHOWED ME HOW MUCH ENERGY SILENCE HAS.

Madonna

WHAT ARE THE BENEFITS?

Rituals help us to shift our attention to where it's most needed. They help to take us out of our busy stream of thoughts and into a quiet space where we feel more in control. Like a reset button for the mind, rituals help us to close all those open tabs and recharge. Cultivating a practice of rituals that you perform at a given time or in a particular situation can help to ground and centre you, better positioning yourself to get on with your day.

People also turn to rituals when faced with situations beyond their control. Research by behavioural scientists at Harvard Business School shows that rituals help with self-control, confidence, motivation, processing emotion, and performance, although benefits will vary depending on what the ritual is trying to achieve. Some benefits could include improved well-being and mood, decreased stress levels, greater energy or concentration and a more positive outlook. You're training your mind and body to take comfort in the ritual, and recognize it as a signal for what comes after. For example, performing a bedtime ritual before sleep is a cue that prompts your body for restorative rest.

WE ARE WHAT WE
REPEATEDLY DO.

Will Durant

DO NOT BE AFRAID TO
DISAPPEAR, FROM IT,
FROM US, FOR A WHILE
AND SEE WHAT COMES
TO YOU IN THE SILENCE.

Michaela Coel

ARE RITUALS
FOR EVERYONE?

Rituals are for anyone and everyone and
can be completely adapted to fit your
lifestyle and schedule. You can practise
as many or as few as you want, and you
can even create your own! Most can
be performed alone, while others are
performed with a partner or in a group.
Since they offer vital headspace and help to
focus the mind, they can help anyone from
any walk of life to approach their day with
a clear head. Developing your own practice
can give you a sense of calmness and
control – something beneficial to us all.

PEACE IS WHEN THE FLOWERS BLOOM.

Amrita Pritam

DON'T LOOK TOO FAR
INTO THE FUTURE,
JUST LOOK AT TOMORROW.
ONE DAY AT A TIME.

Joe Wicks

HOW CAN I MAKE TIME FOR RITUALS?

Try to think about times in your day or week when you have 5 or 10 minutes spare. Is there a time of day when you're sitting on public transport or waiting for something, or a particular time when you often feel frazzled and could use a quick lift? A morning or bedtime ritual is something we can all fit into our lives if we choose to make space and prioritize it. However busy you are, try to commit to fitting in a few meaningful rituals that will help you live more mindfully.

WHAT IF I'M AWAY?

Good question! Most rituals can be performed just about anywhere. If you have a breathing meditation to calm your mind or a morning ritual to set you up for the day, you can perform these on holiday, at a friend's house, in a hotel, on a camping trip... anywhere! This is the beauty of rituals; most are simple and portable! Other more specific rituals – perhaps involving a special place or item – aren't portable, but you could try substituting these practices with something similar. If you're sick or the timing doesn't work out, nothing will be lost by skipping a few days here or there.

THE MORE THAT WE CAN
BRING OUR AUTHENTIC
SELVES... INTO THE
MOMENT, THE MORE
THAT MOMENT WILL
SHOW UP FOR US.

Amanda Gorman

WHERE, WHEN AND HOW OFTEN SHOULD THEY BE DONE?

Your ritual practice is entirely personal to you. You can perform rituals in any way that suits your life and commitments. The obvious place is home, in a quiet space where you can spend a few moments uninterrupted, but you can perform rituals at work or out and about. If you commute to work, your journey could be a time that you use to perform a ritual. If you're an early bird, a morning ritual might make sense to you. Or if food is important to you, mealtimes might be a good choice.

Rituals can be done anywhere, at any time. They should not be a burden, so find a time and space that suits your lifestyle. Rituals can be practised as often or sporadically as you like, however, you will see more benefits if you perform them regularly. A handful of daily rituals can be particularly effective as they set you up mentally and physically for your day. A routine of rituals – for example, a morning, noon, dinnertime and bedtime ritual – can help to scaffold and shape your day.

THE FUNCTION OF
RITUAL... IS TO GIVE FORM
TO HUMAN LIFE, NOT
IN THE WAY OF A MERE
SURFACE ARRANGEMENT,
BUT IN DEPTH.

Joseph Campbell

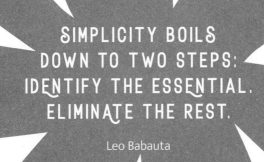

SIMPLICITY BOILS
DOWN TO TWO STEPS:
IDENTIFY THE ESSENTIAL.
ELIMINATE THE REST.

Leo Babauta

WHICH ONES
SHOULD I PICK?

Your ritual practice will evolve naturally.
Pick any that appeal in some way and see
them as a starting point on a journey.
Some you'll want to keep doing; others
you'll prefer to drop. You can try new ones,
add touches or even create your own. If
you end up tweaking them to suit you,
this is ideal; you're listening to your own
needs and responding to what works best
for you. After a ritual, take a moment to
reflect on whether it added value for you
and assess how you feel. Trust your innate
wisdom and develop your own practice.

AIM TO BE THE TRUEST
VERSION OF YOU.
EMBRACE THAT YOU-NESS.
ENDORSE IT. LOVE IT.

Matt Haig

MORNING RITUAL

Wake up with a ritual and it will help to anchor your mood for the rest of the day. This is an excellent habit to get into – setting a purpose to give your day clarity and focus.

First, find a comfortable spot. Take a moment to bring your focus inward. Notice any sensations or tensions and observe your mood. Contemplate an overall intention for the day – not a list of tasks you wish to complete, but something simpler.

For example, an intention might be something like "I will embrace this day" or "I will remember to smile today", or it could be a concept, such as "calmness", "gratitude" or "kindness". Say it out loud if you wish. Commit to living this day in the moment when you can, with a spirit of openness and acceptance. Bring your hands together and give thanks for the day, then continue with your morning with a sense of peace and purpose.

WHEN YOU OPEN YOUR
EYES EACH MORNING,
MAKE SURE YOU
OPEN YOUR HEART.

Sara Ajna

REMEMBER YOU HAVE THE
RIGHT TO BE PROUD.
REMEMBER YOU HAVE
THE RIGHT TO BE YOU.

Dean Atta

THREE THINGS

This ritual is helpful for
cultivating gratitude.

Begin a new journal. Name it *My Feel-Good
Journal* if you like, and write down three
things that you are grateful for today,
or that lift your mood. Reflect on each
in turn, taking time to truly appreciate
what they add to your life and why you
are thankful for them. Express your
gratitude physically, if you like, by bringing
your hands together in front of your
chest and bowing your head, or develop
your own personal gesture of thanks to
perform every time you do this ritual.

NO GESTURE IS TOO
SMALL WHEN DONE
WITH GRATITUDE.

Oprah Winfrey

RECYCLE, REPLENISH, RENEW

This ritual is helpful for letting go of negative emotions or tiredness.

Standing strong and tall, picture your negative feelings as a silk cloak, shrouding the light that shines within you. Now shake your body and shoulders and throw off the cloak, letting it slip gently to the ground. Let anything that is not serving you in this moment fall away. If you prefer a tree image, imagine yourself as an oak in autumn, and let your wilted leaves rustle and fall, replenishing the soil at your feet. Let your light shine and embrace your inner vitality.

LETTING GO GIVES US
FREEDOM... IF, IN OUR
HEART, WE STILL CLING
TO ANYTHING – ANGER,
ANXIETY, OR POSSESSIONS
– WE CANNOT BE FREE.

Thích Nhất Hạnh

COLD SHOWER

This ritual brings your focus inside and into the moment, harnessing your innate power.

Shower as usual at your preferred temperature. Then, turn the shower to run as cold as you can stand. Consciously focus on your in-breath and your out-breath. Count to 30 breaths or repeat "Om Shanti" (which means "peace" in Sanskrit) 30 times. The intensity of the cold water might take your breath away a little, especially if you immerse your head, but it will leave you feeling invigorated and energized.

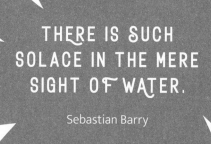

THERE IS SUCH
SOLACE IN THE MERE
SIGHT OF WATER.

Sebastian Barry

FOREST BATHING

Spending time in nature is proven
to carry a host of benefits to our
mental health and our immune
systems. Connecting with trees
and absorbing the power of a
forest is especially therapeutic.

To practise this ritual, walk mindfully
around a park, forest or even your
own garden. Allow yourself to slow
down and embrace the energy of
your environment and the rhythm
of your heart, breathing and strides.
Fully engage with your senses
and surroundings. Breathe in the
healing compounds emitted by
trees and wonder at the wisdom of

these beings that have weathered storms and witnessed history.

Reach out and touch the trunk of a tree. Notice the texture and temperature of the bark. Observe details – knots and buds, beetles and birdsong, colour and movement. Imagine water travelling up the trunk, delivering nutrients from the soil to the leaves, and energy from the sun spreading across its body and down into the ground. See if you can feel connected and part of the system of life. Notice your senses sharpening. Hone in on any sounds, smells or sensations that feel inviting in the moment. To amplify the experience, close your eyes and remove your shoes and socks. Feel your soul being nourished by nature, your mind clear, calm, open and creative.

ALL THAT IS IMPORTANT
IS THIS ONE MOMENT IN
MOVEMENT. MAKE THE
MOMENT IMPORTANT, VITAL,
AND WORTH LIVING.

Martha Graham

RITUAL FOR SELF-LOVE

This ritual, in the spirit of the Japanese concept of *wabi-sabi*, teaches you to accept and learn to love your imperfections. Find a bowl or mug that has hairline cracks or superficial imperfections that don't affect its function. Hold it in your hands and study the imperfections up close. See the beauty in the way each crack has formed and spread. If you have a metallic pen, you could highlight the crack in gold, or draw it on a piece of paper. Understand that we all have quirks and so-called flaws – they are what make us special. Embrace your own imperfections.

RITUAL FOR CLARITY

This ritual will help you see clearly
what it is you need to do.

Choose a fresh essential oil such as
peppermint, cypress or rosemary. Diffuse
three to five drops of it in a burner and
breathe slowly and deeply for a few
moments, focusing on your breath.
Alternatively, brew peppermint tea or
a herbal infusion specifically for clarity.
Mindfully enjoy the scent and taste.
Release any tension in your shoulders and
neck and allow mental fog to clear. Ask
aloud, "What do I need to do?" or "What
do I want?", and let the answers come.

RITUAL AIMS TO IMBUE
THE MUNDANE WITH AN
ELEMENT OF THE MAGICAL.

Maria Popova

RITUAL FOR PROCESSING SADNESS

You could be feeling sad for any number of reasons. Sometimes there's a clear cause, but other times you might not know why you're feeling low. Instead of pushing your sadness away, show it compassion, and it may soften at the edges. Find or buy a plant to symbolize your sadness. Sit with it, and mindfully water and feed it. Tell the plant how you're feeling. Reach out and touch its stem and leaves, noticing its natural beauty and its unique arrangement. When the plant grows, understand this is not your sadness growing; you have enabled sadness to transmute into life.

THE ORDINARY ACTS WE
PRACTISE EVERY DAY
AT HOME ARE OF MORE
IMPORTANCE TO THE SOUL
THAN THEIR SIMPLICITY
MIGHT SUGGEST.

Thomas Moore

MINDFULNESS IS A
PAUSE – THE SPACE
BETWEEN STIMULUS
AND RESPONSE: THAT'S
WHERE CHOICE LIES.

Tara Brach

TO DISCOVER HOW
DEEP OUR ROOTS ARE
IS IMPORTANT.

Bernardine Evaristo

LET GO OF YOUR ANXIETY

Whenever you're feeling anxious, jittery or unsettled, lower your focus to your feet if you're standing, or to your bottom and legs if seated. Let your breathing slow. Allow yourself to be grounded: consciously notice the contact with and support of the ground, floor or chair beneath you, and imagine strong roots reaching down into the earth to stabilize you through any metaphorical weather. Notice your anxiety receding and your mind calming. Embrace the earth's life force building in your legs, travelling up into your abdomen and chest. Let strength replace anxiety.

THERE'S POWER IN
ALLOWING YOURSELF TO
BE KNOWN AND HEARD,
IN OWNING YOUR UNIQUE
STORY, IN USING YOUR
AUTHENTIC VOICE.

Michelle Obama

SMILE FOR JOY

You can perform this ritual alone or share
your smile with others to spread joy.
Consciously soften and lift your eyebrows
until you are smiling gently – a genuine
smile begins with the eyes, not the
mouth. Even if you don't feel like smiling,
allow your face to lift. Bring to mind
a child laughing, or the colour yellow.
Continue to smile, and your smile may
grow. Notice if your mood lifts, too.
Sharing a smile with a friend or stranger
is the simplest gift you can give anyone,
helping both of you feel a connection.

KEEP SMILING, BECAUSE LIFE IS A BEAUTIFUL THING.

Marilyn Monroe

COLOUR SEQUENCE

This is an energizing ritual that can help to rebalance your *qi* or energy, especially when you're feeling tired, sluggish or stressed.

Find a comfortable seated position. Allow your breathing to settle and deepen and softly close your eyes. Bring into your mind the following colour sequence: white, dark blue, green, red, yellow, free colour. Focus on each colour for several slow breaths, moving onto the next when you feel ready. For the final colour, allow your mind to settle on a shade that feels intuitive to you, or that brings you peace.

This is loosely based on a qigong meditative practice, which releases negative emotion from the body and vital organs on your out-breath, and invites in positive energy and calm with each in-breath. For example, you may choose to breathe out anger, anxiety, sadness or fear, and breathe in joy, clarity, creativity or serenity. Don't worry if you find it difficult to visualize each colour; the act of performing this is revitalizing in itself. If you find this rebalancing, consider trying a qigong class that explores this in greater depth, linking in specific organs, sounds, emotions, seasons and elements.

DIVE DEEPER INTO THE
PRESENT, FOR IT IS WHERE
LIFE COMES ALIVE,
INTENSE HUES OF YELLOWS,
GREENS, BLUES, ALL
AWAITING YOUR RETURN.

Satsuki Shibuya

IDIOSYNCRATIC RITUALS
CAN RESTORE OUR
SENSE OF CONTROL
OVER OUR LIVES.

Michael I. Norton

DETOX RITUAL

Great for clearing out sluggishness and detoxing the liver, kidneys and gut, this ritual is particularly helpful during the summer months. Begin by squeezing two lemons and grating the zest of one into a jug. Take time to inhale the fresh, invigorating scent. Add 1–2 tablespoons of raw sugar, honey or sweetener to taste, and add 350 ml of cold water and plenty of ice. Sip slowly and enjoy the vibrant tang of lemon. Imagine the liquid travelling through all the capillaries and cells in your body, clearing out unwanted toxins and leaving your system zingy with vitality.

IF YOU ARE ANXIOUS,
YOU ARE LIVING IN THE
FUTURE. IF YOU ARE AT
PEACE, YOU ARE LIVING
IN THE PRESENT.

Lao Tzu

QUIET THE MIND, AND
THE SOUL WILL SPEAK.

Ma Jaya Sati Bhagavati

YOUR MIND WILL ANSWER MOST QUESTIONS IF YOU LEARN TO RELAX AND WAIT FOR THE ANSWER.

William S. Burroughs

STRESS-BUSTING RITUAL

Got an exam to sit, a presentation to deliver or a big performance coming up? This ritual will help to calm your nerves and alleviate that stress in the minutes before you face your task, so that you are in the right frame of mind to perform to the best of your ability. This is because rituals help to bring a degree of predictability to uncertain situations. They can create a sense of control and constancy, offering us a protective shield against uncertainty and anxiety.

To perform this ritual, stand firm with your feet hip-width apart. Breathing in, arch your spine backward, bring your shoulders back and open your arms with your palms facing forward at shoulder height. Breathing out, hunch forward and bring your hands together in front of your chest. Repeat this ten times, then shake out your arms and legs and say with conviction: "I've got this!" Now, go and nail that task – you have the power, skill and focus. The more you practise this ritual, the greater the signal to your mind that you have it all under control.

THE POWER OF A KEYSTONE
HABIT DRAWS FROM ITS
ABILITY TO CHANGE
YOUR SELF-IMAGE.

Charles Duhigg

PEOPLE NEED TO
WAKE UP TO THEIR
OWN POWER.

Wim Hof

EMBRACING CHANGE

We all encounter change in our lives.
This helps you to embrace the new.
Run a cold tap and let the water flow
over your hands. Bend forward and
splash the water over your face (and
your neck, too, if you like), feeling its
coldness all over you. Notice how you
feel revitalized with the sensation of
cold water on your skin. Give thanks for
this feeling. See the water as the new
element or change that is entering
your life. Welcome it into your world.

STRENGTH IS KNOWING
THAT EVERYONE BELONGS
TO THEMSELVES.

Yaa Gyasi

AS A MAN CHANGES HIS
OWN NATURE, SO DOES THE
ATTITUDE OF THE WORLD
CHANGE TOWARDS HIM.

Mahatma Gandhi

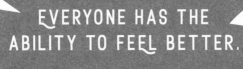

EVERYONE HAS THE
ABILITY TO FEEL BETTER.

Dr Rangan Chatterjee

CANDLE RITUAL

This is an excellent ritual to bring your focus back to a place of quiet strength when your mind feels busy or overwhelmed. It is also effective when you're lacking motivation and want to reignite the fire within you, reminding yourself that you are strong, calm and in control.

Sit cross-legged or kneel before your favourite scented candle or simple tealight. (Try to use soy or beeswax

candles where possible, since they burn cleaner and are more environmentally friendly than paraffin wax candles.) Light the candle, and observe the flame flickering and the wax melt and pool. See how the light dances and moves, and watch any shadows it creates. Focus on the flame and feel the power of that tiny fire inside you, lighting you up with vitality, clarity and purpose. If the candle is scented, allow the scent to transport you to a place that fills you with peace. When you feel ready, blow out the candle and enjoy a moment of stillness.

PEOPLE ARE LIKE STAINED-
GLASS WINDOWS... WHEN
THE DARKNESS SETS IN,
THEIR TRUE BEAUTY IS
REVEALED ONLY IF THERE
IS A LIGHT FROM WITHIN.

Elisabeth Kübler-Ross

YOU HAVE TO LOVE.
YOU HAVE TO FEEL.
IT IS THE REASON YOU
ARE HERE ON EARTH.

Louise Erdrich

TWENTY BREATHS

This is perfect for when you are sitting on a train, tram or bus and have a few minutes to spare.

Zone out from the other passengers and all the busyness going on around you. Bring your focus inward, to the core of your being. Drop your head and look at your hands in your lap or gently close your eyes to avoid distractions. Let sounds wash over you. Allow your breathing to slow and deepen. Count 20 breaths in and 20 breaths out, observing the breath flowing in and out of your body, and focusing on the moment.

IF WE DO EACH THING
CALMLY AND CAREFULLY
WE WILL GET IT DONE
QUICKER AND WITH
MUCH LESS STRESS.

Viggo Mortensen

SLIP INTO SLEEP

This ritual is great for people whose minds are busy fretting as they lie in bed, preventing them from falling into restful sleep.

Lie on your back and gently close your eyes. Allow your back muscles to spread out and melt into your bed. Remember, the mattress is supporting you; you don't need to hold yourself away from it. Now, let your arms and legs slacken. Release any tension or gripping sensation in your hands and

feet, and relax your belly. Allow your neck and head to sink into the mattress.

Relax your shoulders – imagine they are made out of a warm, thick liquid that's spreading across the bed. Release your jaw and cheeks. Let your tongue go slack in your mouth. Feel the skin across your nose and forehead soften, and take a few breaths. Notice if you are frowning a fraction. Gently lift your eyebrows into a soft smile and notice your mood lift and a feeling of contentment and calm wash over you. Allow yourself to drift into a deep, restorative sleep.

FAVOURITE POEM

When you are seeking reassurance
and connection, reading your favourite
poem can ground you and give you the
courage to keep going. If you already have
a favourite poem, great. If not, actively
look up poems until you find one that
really resonates with you. A fairly short,
simple poem works well – one that you
have printed off or copied onto special
paper or a journal page. Read the poem
aloud, paying attention to how the
words sound and any rhythm the poet
has created. Take your time; give the
words space to have an impact on you.

YOU ARE YOUR
BEST THING.

Toni Morrison

CELEBRATING ACHIEVEMENT

It's important to celebrate ourselves, but it's also important to celebrate those around us, too, be they a partner, friend or family member. Form a ring around the person you are celebrating and have a special hat or garland for them to wear. Do a drum roll with your feet, moving up to slapping your palms on your thighs, then clapping your hands and cheering. Express why you're proud of what the person has achieved. Celebrate with a special drink, cake or feast. This cultivates a tradition of sharing when things go well, and circles are an enduring symbol of strength and unity.

RITUAL IS THE PASSAGE
WAY OF THE SOUL
INTO THE INFINITE.

Algernon Blackwood

MIRROR RITUAL

Learn to see the beauty within your soul.
With a spirit of acceptance, look at your
reflection in the mirror. If any criticisms
come to mind, gently push them away.
Imagine you can see through your skin
and flesh to the light and life within. Feel
the radiance and goodness of your soul.
Seek a specific feature to focus on – this
could be a physical feature or a personality
trait. Shine your attention on this feature
and see its beauty. Say aloud, "I love you."

YOU ARE THE LIGHT OF THE WORLD, WHEN YOUR COMPASSION RADIATES AND PERVADES THE WORLD.

Amit Ray

RITUAL FOR FORGIVENESS

The act of forgiving can be difficult.
In order to forgive someone or
something, you need to find compassion.
Carrying around resentment leaves
people drained and strips away their
contentment. Forgiving liberates
you to move on with your life, with
a sense of lightness and, ultimately,
love. It takes courage, for first you
must face your anger or hurt.

Find a leaf, feather or petal to symbolize
whatever it is you wish to forgive.
With a spirit of kindness, think of the

person, behaviour or act that has been taking up negative space in your soul. If there is pain, accept and sit with it a while. Offer it only compassion.

With sincerity in your heart, say, "I forgive you," to the item you have chosen. See the beauty in the object, and be at peace with your decision to forgive. Take your leaf, feather or petal outside and let it blow away in the breeze, taking any resentment with it.

This ritual is powerful because you are taking control of your own mind. It doesn't ignore or diminish wrongdoings; instead, it signals acceptance and willingness to move on.

THE WINDS WILL BLOW
THEIR OWN FRESHNESS
INTO YOU, AND THE STORMS
THEIR ENERGY, WHILE
CARES WILL DROP OFF
LIKE AUTUMN LEAVES.

John Muir

I CAN BE
ANOTHER THING.

Helen Oyeyemi

WRITE A NOTE

Taking a few moments to write a note to a friend or family member is a beautiful way to share kindness with another. Consider what you wish to express. What do you love about this person? When you bring them to mind, what is it that stands out, and what might they need to hear right now? Make sure your words are sincere and come from the heart. Give them the note in person, post it or leave it somewhere they are sure to find it. Your gesture will brighten their day and warm their soul – and yours, too.

NOTHING CAN DIM THE
LIGHT WHICH SHINES
FROM WITHIN.

Maya Angelou

SALUTE THE SUN

This upward salute (*Urdhva Hastasana*) is the first posture of the Sun Salutation (*Surya Namaskar*) in vinyasa yoga. It lifts the body to embrace the sun's life-giving energy and connect with the universe. If you like, this posture can be performed outdoors in the morning, facing east toward the rising sun. With the intent to release in mind, stand with your feet hip-width apart and your arms resting by your sides. On an in-breath, slowly sweep your arms out to the sides and slightly backward, then up and overhead until your palms meet,

with your fingers reaching skyward. Stretch straight up with your arms, reaching through your fingertips. Bring your gaze and your head skyward, too. Slide your shoulders away from your ears, your shoulder blades flattening into your back. Keep your thighs strong, your feet evenly spread, your tailbone tucked and your hips level. Exhale and bring your hands down to a prayer position in front of your chest. Repeat this movement twice more, completing three in total. Give sincere gratitude for the sun for giving life to all living things on earth.

IT'S ALL
ABOUT FREEDOM.

Benjamin Zephaniah

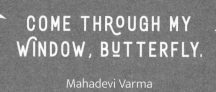

COME THROUGH MY
WINDOW, BUTTERFLY.

Mahadevi Varma

WATER MEDITATION

The sight and sound of water can be
deeply relaxing. If you live near a body
of water, such as an ocean, reservoir,
lake or river, sit beside it and simply
be for 10 minutes. Gaze at the moving
mass of water, allowing your breathing
and mind to settle, and feel a wave of
peace embrace you. Close your eyes
or dip your feet in, if you like, and
become immersed in the moment.

Water flows and forms a large part of our
bodies and planet, and unwinding into a
meditative state beside water is naturally
therapeutic. For first-timers, this can be
a great introduction to meditation.

NOTHING CAN BRING YOU
PEACE BUT YOURSELF.

Ralph Waldo Emerson

BE KIND, FOR
EVERYONE YOU
MEET IS FIGHTING
A HARD BATTLE.

Plato

TENSE AND RELEASE

This ritual is effective for releasing physical and emotional tension.

Lie or sit in a comfortable position. Move slowly around your body, focusing on one area at a time. For example, you could begin with your right foot. Tense the muscles in your foot and count to ten, then release. Now repeat the same for your calf, your shin, your thigh, your glutes. Travel around your body, tensing and releasing every area. As you release, let emotional stress and strain fall away. Often, it can be hard to relax a muscle or release a feeling unless we've flexed it first.

ANY RITUAL IS AN
OPPORTUNITY FOR
TRANSFORMATION.
TO DO A RITUAL, YOU
MUST BE WILLING TO BE
TRANSFORMED IN SOME WAY.

Starhawk

JUST BE KIND. THE
ACT ITSELF, IT'S FREE.
AND IT'S PRICELESS.

Lady Gaga

NOURISHING HAND AND FOOT MASSAGE

When your body's aching after a busy day, this ritual has the power to make you feel much more comfortable and content.

Have your favourite massage oil to hand. Or, to make your own, mix sweet almond carrier oil with a few drops of some essential oils, like lavender, rose, peppermint, sandalwood, sweet orange and sage, adjusting as you prefer. Lay a towel on your chair or floor, light a candle in the room and sit in a comfortable position.

Begin with your left foot. Using small circular movements, thumb pulses, your knuckles, squeezes and sweeping strokes, work around the sole, heel, arch and top of your foot, spending time and care in each area. Notice the feel and scent of the oil. Gently manipulate each toe, tugging and twisting each in turn, remembering to massage the areas between them. Be led by how you feel. Apply more or less pressure as you wish. Repeat for your right foot, your right hand and your left hand.

This self-care therapy is an act of generosity to yourself or others. Massages can reduce anxiety and aid with pain relief, relaxation, emotional regulation and sleep.

WHEN I MEDITATE... I FEEL
THE NEURAL PATHWAYS IN
MY BRAIN OPEN UP... AND
I FEEL MY MOST SHARP.

Katy Perry

REMEMBER TO
BREATHE. IT IS
AFTER ALL, THE
SECRET OF LIFE.

Gregory Maguire

RED LIGHT RITUAL

Instead of worrying about running late,
see a red light as a moment of calm
being offered to you. This is excellent for
turning something you perceived as a
negative into a positive. Every time you
come to a red light, whether you are a
driver, passenger or pedestrian, pause
for a few moments and breathe. Relax
your shoulders, hold your back and neck
straight and meditate on the vibrancy
of the colour red. Be thankful for this
moment that has been gifted to you
before the light turns green. Continue on
your journey with peace in your soul.

ACCEPT WHAT IS, LET GO
OF WHAT WAS, AND HAVE
FAITH IN WHAT WILL BE.

Sonia Ricotti

FREE WRITING

Great for removing mental blockages and allowing self-expression and creativity to flow, free writing is when people write continuously without pausing, usually for a set period of time.

Begin a new notebook or journal and use it just for this ritual. Set a timer for 10 minutes, and simply write. The idea is to let the words flow. Don't worry about spelling, punctuation, grammar or content. Write intuitively if you can, letting your stream of consciousness pour out of you and onto the page. This practice is liberating and can sometimes flag something you didn't even know was subconsciously preoccupying your mind.

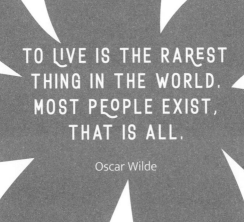

TO LIVE IS THE RAREST
THING IN THE WORLD.
MOST PEOPLE EXIST,
THAT IS ALL.

Oscar Wilde

IF YOU CAN REALLY
OBSERVE YOURSELF FOR
THE DURATION OF A SINGLE
BREATH — YOU WILL
UNDERSTAND IT ALL.

Yuval Noah Harari

SPECIAL PLACE

A special place can provide welcome sanctuary when you need it most. Your special spot might be beside a river, lake or ocean; it could be a woodland glade or a particular rock or tree; or perhaps it's a park bench or town square where you can watch people and wildlife come and go. If it's not practical to go there, try visiting your special place in your mind. Experience its particular appeal and appreciate why it's precious to you. Observe any sights, sounds, smells, textures and tastes you associate with it. Let a feeling of peace envelop you.

SO MANY THINGS
BECOME BEAUTIFUL
WHEN YOU REALLY LOOK.

Lauren Oliver

I RISE EARLY ALMOST EVERY MORNING, AND SIT IN MY CHAMBER, WITHOUT ANY CLOTHES WHATEVER, HALF AN HOUR OR AN HOUR, ACCORDING TO THE SEASON, EITHER READING OR WRITING.

Benjamin Franklin

TEA CEREMONY

This is a calming, affirmative ritual to share with a friend or partner. Although matcha is traditionally used, you can try this with any hot drink. The ritualistic element is important, so always try to use the same small, simple cups or bowls.

Set out your cups, matcha tea-caddy, scoop, whisk and a soft cloth on a clean, cleared table in a quiet place. Boil a kettle and place it on the table. Kneel and take a few slow, respectful breaths. Using the cloth, wipe the cups to symbolically purify them. Scoop the matcha powder into the cups, pour over boiled water and whisk quickly to create froth. In Zen tradition, a sweet can be enjoyed before the tea.

Observe the unique markings of your cup, appreciating any small cracks or imperfections. Take time to sip the tea, noticing its depth of flavour and hue. Sit together in silent contemplation as you give thanks for the rich simplicity of this moment. Bow and express gratitude once you have finished.

The tea ceremony ritual allows you to share the simple act of making and drinking tea while connecting meaningfully with company in an atmosphere of calm – a moment of soul-nourishing respite from the busyness of everyday life.

RITUAL IS A TERRIBLY
IMPORTANT, BINDING
CEMENT IN A SOCIETY.

Alexander McCall Smith

BOX BREATHING

This breathing ritual can very quickly help your mind feel calm and clear, and is especially effective in times of anxiety or stress. It can also help alleviate brain fog, negative emotions and anger.

Breathe in for a count of four, hold for four, breathe out for four, and hold for four, all through your nose. Visualize a calming square as you breathe. Repeat for as many rounds as you like. Lengthening your out-breath helps you relax more deeply, both mentally and physically. For extended breathing, inhale for four, hold for four, exhale for six, and hold for two.

WORD OF THE DAY

This ritual reminds you to be
playful and creative.

Have someone choose a word for you or
pick a word at random from a newspaper
or book. The more unusual the word, the
better. The challenge is to use this word
today in a conversation with someone.
If you manage to get it in several times,
even better! This is a reminder that life
is full of opportunities for fun and for
personal growth. Practising rituals doesn't
have to be serious; there's always space
for playfulness. You might need a little
inventiveness to steer the conversation
so you can use your word – a great
chance to embrace your creativity!

THERE ARE LONG
SECONDS ALL OVER THE
PLACE. WE JUST DON'T
ALWAYS NOTICE THEM.

Joanna Cannon

AFFIRMATIONS

Curate a handful of affirmations that strongly resonate with you and work in a variety of situations. When you need each one, say it clearly with conviction three times. Visualize a bubble of strength and confidence surrounding you. You've got this!

Example affirmations include:

- I am capable, I am calm
- Today I choose kindness
- Breathe in the positive, let go of the negative
- I accept this day and all that it brings
- I forgive and peacefully detach from hurt
- Release, ground, love

HOPE IS BEING ABLE
TO SEE THAT THERE
IS LIGHT DESPITE ALL
OF THE DARKNESS.

Desmond Tutu

IT'S THE REPETITION OF
AFFIRMATIONS THAT LEADS
TO BELIEF. AND ONCE
THAT BELIEF BECOMES A
DEEP CONVICTION, THINGS
BEGIN TO HAPPEN.

Muhammad Ali

SHE DIDN'T JUST STACK THE WOOD, SHE STACKED THE WOOD IN A PATTERN.

Louise Erdrich

DECLUTTERING RITUAL

It can be difficult to relax in a cluttered space, as all the mess signals tasks we've yet to deal with. As well as being therapeutic, decluttering can be an excellent exercise in mindfulness.

Find a 5-minute slot in your day and use this to tackle a specific area of your house or workspace. You could target a kitchen shelf, your bedside table or your desk, for example. Be present in the moment and notice the textures and details of the items you're handling. Reflect on what each item is adding to your life. If anything no longer serves you, you could donate or recycle it.

IT'S ONLY WHEN YOU
HITCH YOUR WAGON TO
SOMETHING LARGER
THAN YOURSELF THAT
YOU REALIZE YOUR
TRUE POTENTIAL.

Barack Obama

FULL MOON RITUAL

Whether it's a clear night or whether the moon is obscured by cloud cover, feel its regulating power and rhythm. The moon controls the oceans, and you're made up of 70 per cent water, too! Watch or visualize the moon and its calming presence in the night sky. Be grateful for the light and energy from the sun, reflecting off the moon and reaching us on earth, providing light by which to navigate at night. Take a few minutes to acknowledge your place in the universe. Embrace the coming lunar cycle and give thanks for the one that's ending.

THE ONLY TRUE VOYAGE
OF DISCOVERY... WOULD BE
NOT TO VISIT STRANGE
LANDS BUT TO POSSESS
OTHER EYES, TO BEHOLD
THE UNIVERSE THROUGH
THE EYES OF ANOTHER.

Marcel Proust

BEING THE BEST YOU

What's stopping you from being
your best, most compassionate
self? The truth is... nothing!

To amplify and focus your energy on your
finest qualities, speak this aloud to the
universe: "Help me have the courage to be
the very best version of me." Then, take this
sentiment into your heart. Feel it. Mean it. You
are free to be that version of yourself from
this moment forward, and to let your best
traits flourish. Embrace that freedom and the
deep sense of empowerment and serenity
it brings. If you slip up from time to time,
that's OK. Every version of yourself is worthy
of space. Accept your flaws; we're all human.

MY APPROACH IS
JUST FEARLESS.

Stormzy

YOU ONLY NEED ONE RAY OF LIGHT TO CHASE ALL THE SHADOWS AWAY.

Fredrik Backman

WHEN THINGS DON'T GO YOUR WAY

If you're someone who carries frustration or irritation with you long after something doesn't go your way, this practice can help you to move on.

As honestly as you can, write down exactly what is upsetting you on a scrap of paper. If you can't express how you feel, you could use key words such as "angry", "annoyed", "hurt", "embarrassed" or "disappointed", or draw a doodle or emoji to represent it. In a large, flame-proof bowl or bucket, set fire to the scrap of paper and turn your frustration to ash. Notice how much better you feel after letting it all go.

DIFFERENT
VIEW RITUAL

This helps to develop and
practise empathy.

Take a moment to think of something
that happened recently and how you
responded to it. Now try to see the same
event from a different point of view. For
example, if someone pulled out in front
of you, place yourself in that person's
shoes. Why did they pull out? Were they
running late? What for? If somebody
snubbed, ignored or seemed rude to
you, is it possible they didn't see you
or could have been preoccupied with

their own worries? Consider whether you could try to see things from other perspectives more regularly.

To help with this, go outside and find a stone. Study it from one angle. Notice its unique dips, marks and colours. Run your thumb over the surface and feel the texture and weight in your hand. Turn the stone over and look at it from a different angle: it's the same stone, but you're seeing a different side to it. Next time you find yourself becoming irritated with a situation, recall this ritual and commit to seeing it from another point of view. You are practising empathy and not jumping to ungrounded or irrational assumptions. This practice serves you and your precious headspace, and others involved.

LIFE DOESN'T CHANGE,
BUT YOUR PERCEPTION
DOES. IT'S ALL ABOUT
WHAT YOU FOCUS ON.

Wim Hof

BEDTIME RITUAL

Preparing mentally and physically for bed is one of the simplest and best things you can do to protect your well-being. Create your own ritual as you prefer, ensuring as part of it you turn off all gadgets and screens an hour before you plan to sleep. Keep lighting to a minimum – nightfall has primed our brains and bodies for sleep for millennia while modern lighting and tech interfere with those natural rhythms. Something relaxing – a 10-minute yoga sequence or simply washing your feet and face – is an ideal practice for bedtime. You could also write a few words about your day and a hope for tomorrow in your journal. If anything is on your mind, putting it on paper will help you to switch off.

BLOCK OUT ALL THE
NEGATIVE ENERGY,
AND JUST LOVE.

Ariana Grande

PUT YOUR THOUGHTS TO
SLEEP, DO NOT LET THEM
CAST A SHADOW OVER
THE MOON OF YOUR HEART.
LET GO OF THINKING.

Rumi

IN THIS MOMENT, THERE
IS PLENTY OF TIME. IN
THIS MOMENT, YOU ARE
PRECISELY AS YOU SHOULD
BE. IN THIS MOMENT, THERE
IS INFINITE POSSIBILITY.

Victoria Moran

MAKE YOUR BED

Perhaps this sounds like a parent nagging you, but there's wisdom in the simple ritual of making your bed every morning. With care and reverence, straighten out your sheets and tuck them tightly underneath the mattress. Fluff your duvet and lay it back down. Puff up your pillows and place them against the headboard. Add any special touches you like, conducting each act mindfully. Spend a few moments giving gratitude for a warm, comfortable bed to sleep in. When night falls, you can return to a crisp, beautifully made bed – much more inviting than crumpled sheets – and get the peaceful sleep you deserve.

LUNCHTIME RITUAL

Turn the act of eating into a ritual and work on improving your relationship with food. This practice can grow your appreciation of how and what you eat on a deeper level. Mindfully prepare a simple lunch – a fresh salad is ideal, or something else you'd enjoy. Pay attention as you prepare your meal. As you chew, observe the flavours and textures. Breathe in the aroma of your food, and think about where it came from. Appreciate each bite. Take your time. Be grateful for the sustenance your lunch has given you. Give thanks for the food, soil, sun and water that nourishes you.

THE STRUCTURE OF
ROUTINE COMFORTS US,
AND THE SPECIALNESS OF
RITUAL VITALIZES US.

Maria Popova

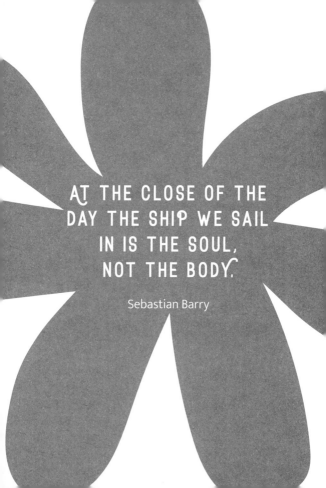

AT THE CLOSE OF THE
DAY THE SHIP WE SAIL
IN IS THE SOUL,
NOT THE BODY.

Sebastian Barry

THERE'S SOMEBODY WHO'S
GOING TO LIKE YOU; YOU
DON'T NEED TO TWIST
YOURSELF INTO SHAPES.

Chimamanda Ngozi Adichie

SOUND JOURNEY

Immersing yourself in healing sounds can be transformative, helping you feel powerfully connected to yourself and the universe.

Find a recording that resonates with your soul – there are many available on music and video apps. Search for healing, meditation, spiritual, gong or solfeggio tracks. For example, there are 528 Hz tracks for positive transformation that can be found online, which studies have shown to have stress-reducing effects. You could also try birdsong, jungle or ocean sounds, or world music with indigenous percussion. Once you've found a track you like, find a comfortable position lying or sitting, and gently close your eyes. Allow the soundwaves to wash over you and carry away anything that doesn't serve you. Allow your entire body and soul to be immersed in the sound experience, or, as some people call it, sound bathing. Let any visuals or sensations you experience, however unusual or intense, play out. When the track ends, slowly open your eyes, wiggle your fingers and toes and gradually return to your day feeling revitalized. Give thanks for the music. This practice can be deeply healing on a spiritual level.

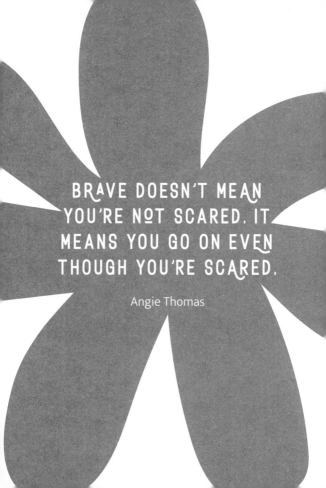

BRAVE DOESN'T MEAN
YOU'RE NOT SCARED. IT
MEANS YOU GO ON EVEN
THOUGH YOU'RE SCARED.

Angie Thomas

TO BE BEAUTIFUL
MEANS TO BE YOURSELF.
YOU DON'T NEED TO
BE ACCEPTED BY
OTHERS. YOU NEED TO
ACCEPT YOURSELF.

Thích Nhất Hạnh

SHAKE IT!

This ritual is all about shaking
out your inhibitions.

Choose a track that feels upbeat and
happy to you. Turn the volume up and
dance around an open space, moving
in any way that feels intuitive. If there's
a particular dance routine for your
chosen song, you may prefer to do that.
Let joy, energy and playfulness pour
out of you. Enjoy the warmth in your
skin, the feeling of your heart beating
faster and the movement of your feet.
Embrace this moment of exhilaration
every time you need a quick lift and
a reminder that there are always
opportunities for fun in your life.

YOUR GAZE OUTWARD IS
SO MUCH MORE IMPORTANT
THAN THE GAZE ON YOU.

Jojo Moyes

RITUAL FOR GRIEF OR LOSS

This ritual involves confronting and sitting with your grief or pain. Prepare for the emotions you might face and perform this when you're feeling strong.

Find a large, smooth stone to represent your sadness or loss, or if it is a particular person or animal you are grieving, choose something that represents them for you – a favourite belonging of theirs, for instance. Cradle it lovingly in your hands while you think about the person or object you have lost. Really bring them to mind and connect with them in your spirit. Feel love radiating out from your being, enveloping both of you. If there's pain and tears, let them come. There's absolutely no shame in crying – remember all of your emotions deserve to be processed.

If you have selected a stone, you could draw a picture or write a message on it. Let this be intuitive and relevant to the person or thing you are grieving. Take the stone and place it in a favourite spot. Or, if you've chosen a special belonging, return it to its place. Performing rituals after experiencing loss can help to alleviate feelings of grief. Mentally processing an action to address the loss can help you to feel better, regaining an element of control.

COME! LET US TAKE
A MOMENT'S SHELTER
UNDER SOME ROOF.

Amrita Pritam

GLOWS AND GROWS

A lovely ritual to share with family or friends around the dinner table, this teaches us to recognize and appreciate moments of value together, creating a space for gratitude and sharing. Everyone can join in with this evening practice.

Each person shares something from their day that they see as a "glow" – something that has lifted their spirits. They then share something they consider a "grow" – a thing they found challenging or could learn from. They could also add a "hello" at the end – something they're looking forward to. Pass a talisman round the table for each person to hold on their turn. This creates a space where all contributions can be heard and respected.

LOVING KINDNESS

Choose to spread compassion and you will illuminate the lives of all in your world, including yourself.

It's common to make assumptions about people we encounter day to day, even if we don't intend to, and often these assumptions can be critical. Even just thinking uncharitable thoughts can be toxic, so learning to cultivate a mindset of kindness and love can really help you to become less judgmental. At the same time, this practice can improve how you see yourself – as inherently kind.

Commit to approaching your day with kindness. Prime yourself to actively look for the good in new people you meet, rather than focusing on perceived negatives. Repeat the mantra, "I am filled with loving kindness", five times, and mean it. Now go out and practise what you preach! Channel compassion toward everyone you encounter and notice how much better it can make you feel.

To include a meditation at the end of your day, imagine you are filled with compassionate energy or *qi*. Radiate waves of loving kindness to all the people in your life. With practice, you should be able to extend this to make peace with those you find especially challenging. This is ultimately better for you and your headspace.

NEVER UNDERESTIMATE
THE BIG IMPORTANCE
OF SMALL THINGS.

Matt Haig

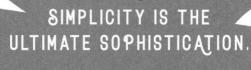

SIMPLICITY IS THE
ULTIMATE SOPHISTICATION.

Leonardo da Vinci

PEBBLE RITUAL

This is a symbolic act for manifesting
a particular objective.

Take a pebble or crystal that is especially
appealing to you. Before you begin,
place it in sunlight so it is bathed in
solar energy. Holding it in your left
hand, ask for its help in some particular
way. For example, you could ask it to
help you finish an assignment, support
a friend who is struggling or help
guide you through a difficult decision.

Or you could ask the stone to help you unwind, overcome a particular fear, express yourself honestly or see some aspect of your life with clarity.

Feel the surface of the stone and notice its unique features – like fingerprints, no two stones are exactly alike. Does it have pits, marks or layers, and is it translucent or opaque? Appreciate its innate power and beauty, embodying the energy of the universe. Feel its protective shield holding you in safety and peace.

HAPPINESS IS ABOUT PEACE.

Jada Pinkett Smith

EVERY DAY,
WE WRITE
THE FUTURE.

Amanda Gorman

THE LITTLE THINGS?
THE LITTLE MOMENTS?
THEY AREN'T LITTLE.

Jon Kabat-Zinn

CONCLUSION

Committing to a ritual is devoting a few minutes of precious time to yourself. It's respecting and safeguarding your inner peace in a busy world, leaving you better equipped to handle the challenges of everyday life. Since rituals are imbued with deeper meaning beyond just a sequence of actions, they signify moments of importance, helping us to navigate our lives.

Hopefully the tips within this book will have inspired you to begin your own exploration into the power of rituals, leading you to discover and develop new relationships with yourself and the world around you.

Meditations for Every Day

Hardback

ISBN: 978-1-80007-676-1

Even in the rush of the busiest days, there is a way to press pause on life's pressures and find a stillness within. Meditation is the key. Whether you're completely new to the practice or just looking for a dose of further inspiration, this book of tips and quotations will help you establish a long-lasting and soul-nourishing habit.

Spirituality for Every Day

Hardback

ISBN: 978-1-80007-438-5

For many, spirituality is a difficult concept to grasp. But the good news is anyone can understand and cultivate it. Packed with comforting quotes and simple but effective tips, this soothing little book will help you on your journey to a more positive and peaceful life.

Have you enjoyed this book?
If so, find us on Facebook at
Summersdale Publishers, on Twitter
at **@Summersdale** and on Instagram
at **@summersdalebooks** and get in
touch. We'd love to hear from you!

www.summersdale.com